GOLF

The Worst Game You'll Ever Love

MATT WOLFF

8102 Lemont Road, #300
Woodridge, IL 60517
Phone: 630-390-3580   Fax: 630-390-3585

Copyright © 2003 Great Quotations, Inc.

Compiled by Matt Wolff

Cover Design by Design Dynamics
Illustrations by Michael Mckee

Published by Great Quotations Publishing Co.,

Library of Congress Catalog Card Number : 98-075785

ISBN: 1-56245-363-7

Printed in Hong Kong 2003

This collection of humorous

quotations and cartoons is dedicated

to the millions of golfers who have

known the thrill of victory and the

agony of three feet.

JUST OFF THE 16TH FAIRWAY, RODNEY JEFFERSON HAS A DISCUSSION WITH HIS CADDIE.

SOLICITING THE LOCAL PRO ...FROSTY SEEKS THE ANSWER TO WHY HIS ARMS KEEP FLYING OFF IN MID-SWING.

THE DAY WAS FILLED WITH PROMISE...UNTIL THE 4TH HOLE WHEN CHAD TRIED TO PLAY A SHOT FROM THE WATER.

"**A**lways throw clubs ahead of you. That way you don't have to waste energy going back to pick them up."

TOMMY BOLT

"**Y**ou've just one problem. You stand too close to the ball — after you've hit it."

SAM SNEAD, to a pupil

"**I** have three-putted in over forty countries."

FRED CORCORAN

"**I**f profanity had an influence on the flight of the ball, the game would be played far better than it is."

HORACE G. HUTCHINSON

7

DORA
DUFFNAGLE
AND HER CADDIE
HANDLE A
DIFFICULT
UPHILL LIE.

"I'M GLAD WE'RE PLAYING THE TOP NINE TODAY... THAT BOTTOM NINE IS REALLY HELL!"

"Putting isn't golf. Greens should be treated almost the same as water hazards: you land on them, then add two strokes to your score."

CHI CHI RODRIGUEZ

"Real golfers don't use naked-lady tees."

"The way I putted, I must've been reading the greens in Spanish and putting them in English."

HOMERO BLANCAS,
Mexican-American Professional

"Real golfers, whatever the provocation, never strike a caddie with the driver. The sand wedge is far more effective."

HUXTABLE PIPPEY

Saint Peter knocks in the 42,754th ace of his illustrious career.

WENDELL LEARNS NOT TO LEAVE THE TEE AREA UNTIL EVERYONE HAS HIT.

"**Y**ou know the old rule: 'He who have fastest cart never have to play bad lie.'"

MICKEY MANTLE

"**P**ick the ball up, have the clubs destroyed, and leave the course."

VISCOUNT CASTLEROSSE,
British columnist, to his caddie after topping
three straight shots.

"It took me seventeen years to get three thousand hits in baseball. I did it in one afternoon on the golf course."

HANK AARON

"My worst day on the golf course still beats my best day in the office."

CHESTER
BUMBLEBURG
GOT ALL
UNGLUED OVER
A FOUR-FOOTER
FOR PAR.

AFTER THE ACCIDENTAL CLUBBING OF MRS. WINKLEMAN, MR. WINKLEMAN TAKES A TWO STROKE PENALTY AND PLAYS THRU.

"Nothing goes down
slower than a golf
handicap."

BOBBY NICHOLS

"Mulligan: invented by
an Irishman who wanted
to hit one more twenty-
yard grounder."

> "**I**f I'da cleared the trees
> and drove the green,
> it woulda been a great
> tee shot."

SAM SNEAD

> "**I**f I swung the gavel the
> way I swung that golf
> club, the nation would
> be in a helluva mess."

TIP O'NEILL

GILBERT TOOK
AIM AT WHAT
WAS TO BE HIS
LAST SHOT OF
THE DAY.

"THE GREENS
SEEM A LITTLE
SLOW TODAY,
ETHEL...IT MUST
BE RAINING."

"**I** am the most over-taught and under-learned golfer in the U.S.A."

HERB GRAFFIS

"**P**rayer never seems to work for me on the golf course. I think this has something to do with my being a terrible putter."

REV. BILLY GRAHAM

"**R**eal golfers don't cry when they line up their fourth putt."

"**G**olf is the hardest game in the world to play and the easiest to cheat at."

DAVE HILL

AFTER INNUMERABLE SWINGS AT THE BUNKERED BALL, HARVEY IS REDUCED TO THE USELESS PRODUCTION OF "SAND ANGELS."

Mrs. Duffnagle takes a free drop!

"**H**ook: the addiction of
fifty percent of all
golfers.
Slice: the weakness of
the other half."

JIM BISHOP

"**N**o matter how hard I
try, I just can't seem to
break sixty-four."

JACK NICKLAUS

"**G**imme: an agreement between two losers who can't putt."

JIM BISHOP

"**G**ive me a millionaire with a bad backswing and I can have a very pleasant afternoon."

GEORGE LOW

"I'LL BE **DAMNED** IF I'M CHASING THAT ONE, MYRTLE."

ALL HIS LIFE, CHESTER BURNBALL CLAIMED HE WAS A 35 HANDICAP.

"**R**eal golfers never question their client's score."

"**R**eal golfers have two handicaps: one for braggin' and one for bettin'."

"**N**ever bet with anyone
you meet on the first tee
who has a deep suntan,
a one-iron in his bag
and squinty eyes."

DAVE MARR

"**M**y car absolutely will
not run unless my golf
clubs are in the trunk."

BRUCE BERLET

"HIT THAT ONE A LITTLE FAT, HUH, CHESTER?"

THE RESULTS OF OVERSWING.

"**T**he golf swing is like
sex. You can't be
thinking about the
mechanics of the act
while you're performing."

DAVE HILL

"**T**he only thing that
you should force in a golf
swing is the club back
into the bag."

BYRON NELSON

"There's an old saying:
If a man comes home
with sand in his cuffs
and cockleburs in his
pants, don't ask him
what he shot."

SAM SNEAD

"Golferswhotalkfastswingfast."

BOB TOSKI

WILMA'S FIRST PAR!

"**N**o one who ever had
lessons would have a
swing like mine."

LEE TREVINO

"**I** still swing the way I
used to, but when I look
up the ball is going in a
different direction."

LEE TREVINO

"**O**ver the years, I've studied habits of golfers. I know what to look for. Watch their eyes. Fear shows up when there is an enlargement of the pupils. Big pupils lead to big scores."

SAM SNEAD

"**N**o matter what happens — never give up a hole. . . . In tossing in your cards after a bad beginning you also undermine your whole game, because to quit between tee and green is more habit-forming than drinking a highball before breakfast."

SAM SNEAD

"**I**'m playing like Tarzan
— and scoring like Jane."

CHI CHI RODRIGUEZ

"**G**olf is a game in
which you yell 'fore',
shoot six, and write
down five."

PAUL HARVEY, news commentator
Golf Digest, 1979

THE TEN
COMMANDMENTS
OF GOLF

COMMANDMENT

Thou shalt playeth the ball from wherst it lies!

COMMANDMENT

hou shalt not relieve your-self upon the landscape.

Thou shalt not maketh sand castles in the bunker!

COMMANDMENT

Thou shalt not agitate the indigenous fowl!

V

COMMANDMENT

Thou shalt not removeth a ball from the cup with your mouth!

VI

COMMANDMENT

Thou shalt not poppeth wheelies with thy golf cart.

VII

COMMANDMENT

Thou shalt not excavate your ball from the bowels of a hazard without the proper weaponry.

Thou shalt not covet thy neighbor's ball!

IX

COMMANDMENT

Thou shalt stop playing whenst **I** say so!

COMMANDMENT

Honor thy caddie, for he knoweth the way!

Other Titles by Great Quotations, Inc.

Hard Covers

Ancient Echoes
Behold the Golfer
Commanders in Chief
The Essence of Music
First Ladies
Good Lies for Ladies
Great Quotes From Great Teachers
Great Women
I Thought of You Today
Journey to Success
Just Between Friends
Lasting Impressions
My Husband My Love
Never Ever Give Up
The Passion of Chocolate
Peace Be With You
The Perfect Brew
The Power of Inspiration
Sharing the Season
Teddy Bears
There's No Place Like Home

Paperbacks

301 Ways to Stay Young
ABC's of Parenting
Angel-grams
African American Wisdom
Astrology for Cats
Astrology for Dogs
The Be-Attitudes
Birthday Astrologer
Can We Talk
Chocoholic Reasonettes
Cornerstones of Success
Daddy & Me
Erasing My Sanity
Graduation is Just the Beginning
Grandma I Love You
Happiness is Found Along the Way
Hooked on Golf
Ignorance is Bliss
In Celebration of Women
Inspirations
Interior Design for Idiots

Great Quotations, Inc.
8102 Lemont Road, #300
Woodridge, IL 60517
Phone: 630-390-3580   Fax: 630-390-3585

Other Titles by Great Quotations, Inc.

Paperbacks

I'm Not Over the Hill
Life's Lessons
Looking for Mr. Right
Midwest Wisdom
Mommy & Me
Mother, I Love You
The Mother Load
Motivating Quotes
Mrs.Murphy's Laws
Mrs. Webster's Dictionary
Only A Sister
The Other Species
Parenting 101
Pink Power
Romantic Rhapsody
The Secret Langauge of Men
The Secret Langauge of Women
The Secrets in Your Name
A Servant's Heart
Social Disgraces
Stress or Sanity
A Teacher is Better Than
Teenage of Insanity
Touch of Friendship
Wedding Wonders
Words From the Coach

Perpetual Calendars

365 Reasons to Eat Chocolate
Always Remember Who Loves You
Best Friends
Coffee Breaks
The Dog Ate My Car Keys
Extraordinary Women
Foundations of Leadership
Generations
The Heart That Loves
The Honey Jar
I Think My Teacher Sleeps at School
I'm a Little Stressed
Keys to Success
Kid Stuff
Never Never Give Up
Older Than Dirt
Secrets of a Successful Mom
Shopoholic
Sweet Dreams
Teacher Zone
Tee Times
A Touch of Kindness
Apple a Day
Golf Forever
Quotes From Great Women
Teacher Are First Class